ESSEX CLAY

Essex Clay

ANDREW MOTION

FABER & FABER

First published in 2018
by Faber & Faber Ltd
Bloomsbury House
74–77 Great Russell Street
London WC1B 3DA
This paperback edition first published in 2019

Typeset by Hamish Ironside
Printed in the UK by TJ International Ltd, Padstow, Cornwall

A CIP record for this book is available from the British Library

ISBN 978-0-571-33997-6

10 9 8 7 6 5 4 3 2 1

Gillian Motion 1928–1978

and

Richard Motion 1921–2006

Acknowledgements

Acknowledgements and thanks are due to *The Echo Chamber* (BBC Radio 4), on which a part of this poem was broadcast in December 2017.

Contents

PART ONE   3

PART TWO   65

PART THREE   87

ESSEX CLAY

PART ONE

The intact frost of early morning
    and a blade of ice
        drawn from the tap in the stable yard.

The village as they drive through
        half asleep under twisting chimneys.

The church   Victorian Doomsday
    moored to the hilltop edge
        with its pretty flotilla of graves.

The weathervane cockerel's gold and flying eye.

The lane
    straightening beside water meadows
        under a thatch of bare chestnuts
            shattered with daylight.

Gravel in the ford
        washed by the brimming stream
    the Blackwater
and pebbles magnified   tawny   beach colours
    with that other river   the river of shining tar
        shivering underneath.

Last night's snowdust
    in suddenly wide-open ploughed fields.

Flints like hip bones and knee bones.

    Clay clods supporting
miniature drift-triangles on their windward side.

His mother silent beside him
        her yellow hair trapped and placid in a hairnet

her clean cream jodhpurs   red collar   black riding jacket

        her stock like a bandage

                her gold pin
                        adorned with the mask of a fox.

                                *

He is seventeen   confident   opinionated
                and definitely at odds
                                on this subject at least.

                He does not approve.

        But   when he glances into the footwell
and sees his mother's narrow feet
                        fluffy sheepskin slippers
                        paddling by turns at the brake
                                accelerator   clutch
        he is silent.

He cannot bring himself
                to have that argument again.

                                *

        In the car park of the White Hart
                        also the bus stop
he reminds himself

        [6]

no one makes a scene   not at his age

and condescends   tips his head a little
to kiss his mother goodbye.

A skim of skin
is enough.

But he does see and cannot forget her hairnet in close-up
a black cobweb   tougher of course

and feels it
scratch
the tip of his nose.

Then he is out in the wind buttoning his overcoat
the ankle-length   topsoil-brown   itchy
war-time soldier's greatcoat
the British Warm
borrowed from his father's wardrobe
without permission
stolen actually
which makes him   beside his holdall
a soldier himself
he imagines.

*

Exactly as his mother grinds the Hillman back into gear
the silhouette of his bus
bulges over the hilltop beyond the White Hart.

He flinches away
to discover his mother's face is

already no longer her face
          but an after-image
       hovering a little way behind her
as she guns the engine   and wriggles into
     the traffic flow.

     Her exhaust plume rapidly fades into the spectre of
        a spectre.

Dark petrol-dribbles escaping the pipe
          might well be a trail of crumbs
               dot-dot-dot all the way home.

                              *

     The bus is almost past him now   except
when he hoists his arm
     the whole snow-filthy bulk amazingly

                                        stops.

Double doors hiss open.

          Cigarette fug flops out.

And in he steps
     with too many hands
          or not enough hands
to pay the fare
     to manage the bloody holdall
          to hold   tight.

     It's OK sonny it's OK.

[8]

Twirling up to the top deck
        stumbling as the bus surges and sashays
            forward
                with a shudder through every one of its
                    body plates
he lurches for a last glimpse of the lane back to the
    village
        and finds no car in sight.

                            *

From this height
        smearing the window mist with his sleeve
            the whiskery sleeve that makes an O
        fringed with delicate nettle-hair scratch marks
he can see across a whole cabbage field
        creased with snow.

        And no one the entire journey
        to notice even   let alone ridicule
            either the relief
                or the alarm of solitude
he reveals by leaning his head against the glass
                on the trembling chill
        and pretending he is asleep.

Although   despite appearances
        he is still watching in fact   vaguely
the shadow of the bus shrink
        where it meets a burst of heavy snow
                then elongate as the snow weakens

so one minute he sees himself not at all
        the next topples forward across hedgerows
        brick walls
                window panes
                        cars shawled at the curbside
                                shop fronts   mannequins
                                    slopes of threadbare winter wheat

and below this the clay six feet deep
                malevolent pasty face
                        ash smears and ochre
a dead weight but in fact alive
        sluggishly
                waiting with all the time in the world
to sculpt its lead around gumboots and plough blades
                    to rear and obliterate whatever it can

until an hour has gone and the bus flusters
        into Sawbridgeworth
                    where its shadow abruptly
        falls in through the windows and sinks down
                among the other shadows already assembled
                        and is absorbed.

                            *

Clambering out
                    holdall thumping the door
he forgets himself
            the instant he sets eyes upon her.

Juliet.

    Her face and love-name coinciding.

Her black hair   black
              not a black enough word.

              Her red mouth.

        Her skin white   but mainly full
              ripeness.

And she is looking straight at him.

        She is.

              Glittering and
        ignoring her fluttery mother beside her
which he should not.

        He shakes her mother's hand
headscarf   specs   face-fuzz powder.

        But for Juliet

              their cheeks brush-collide
and he smells
                    mint.

        Should have thought of that.

Never mind.
              Just find the car
                    boot tricky
                    crammed already
with a clutch of decapitated shopping-bag fledglings.

        It's OK sonny it's OK.

Then next question.

     Front seat or back.

     Back.

But hunching forward   laying one forearm flat
    on pale-green clammy plastic
Juliet's black hair a swelling wave
    trapped inside her collar
       until they set off

       and the heater cranks up

and Juliet
      slips her hand
    inside this wave of black to set it free
     and it flood-slithers
over the shoulders of her coat onto his hand
     which jolts in the electric shock.

               *

    Afternoon   already   somehow
and Juliet's mother has disappeared thank you God
     she has work to do
   while   despite the cold
the clouds and snow flurries
    shovelling west from Siberia
      he and Juliet leave the house for a walk.

He spares a thought for his own mother.

Will she be home already
                    defeated
she would say that
                    defeated
                              by cold.

Her voice stays with him through the back yard
        ghosting

                        boiler shed
ghosting
                        dog kennel
ghosting
                        wood shed
ghosting.

        But he cannot hear what the ghost says.

                              *

They step from the lee of the house
              immediately into ice puffs
where cold slits his eyes

        and he sees ahead   guesses rather
a dead prairie sprinkled with snowstones
              his greatcoat
                    not so ridiculous now

        no more than Juliet's white fur hat and
Afghan or   Doctor Zhivago number
        fur blustering at collar and wrists
              while she butts into the wind

                    arms folded tight   hugging herself
        one blue vein pulsing in her porcelain neck.

                                        *

As for his own face
            he cannot   dare not
        what with eyes streaming   whole face
stiff like a stroke   but still
        blathering   this and that
                    this and that
            their destination of all things
next year's Christmas trees
                    dimly darkening the horizon.

                                        *

        Well
                    they do ask for it farmers
                ripping everything out
        hedges   hundreds of years
                    shelter.

                                        *

            And yet he still does manage
to lead her on.

                    As she leads him
        down the long narrow headland

snowflakes glued on the winter wheat shoots
  dithering beside them.

     *

Jesus though
  laughable this cold
   laughable and
suddenly it gets the better of him.

So he veers
   leaf blown
     back the way they came.

But Juliet is deliberately standing in his way.

    And his mouth
  did she mean this
   obviously she meant this
   his mouth
blurs runnily back to life in the warmth of her mouth.

   For a moment there is

pure darkness.

   Pure slippery deepening wet dark.

   And heat
as his hand slides inside her coat.

Astounding radiator heat.

When he touches bare skin
        between the waist of her jeans and her jersey
and Juliet slides her mouth from his mouth to his ear
        where she pours into him
                the blaze of his own name.

                                        *

                He wants her now.

He wants her
        among the snowdropped wheat tips
and flints
        gleaming between the seed drills.

        In the slicing snow swipes.

Under the weightless silk cloud sheet.

        A perfectly ridiculous idea.

Although
        when they bow towards the house
                arms looping each other's shoulders
against the wind opposing
        they realise   what they have promised each other.

                                        *

There is an hour before they must change
                                        for the party.

Juliet insists
>they have to go.

After she has dragged the curtains shut
after she has lit the fire
>after she has flicked through her box of LPs and
>>chosen
>>>*Music from Big Pink*

>>soul mate

>he stands to one side of the room by the curtains
>>>a proper   young   man
beside the floor-length wall-to-wall expensive blue
>velvet curtains
>>>with snow falling outside
>>>and agrees.

>>>Of course they must.

>He stares flagrantly at her in the armchair
>>to show he would rather not.

>Knees drawn up   legs curled round like
>>a mermaid on a rock

>not that

>>>like herself
>>>right hand shielding her eyes
>>concentrating on 'The Weight'
>>>*I pulled in to Nazareth*
left hand   square-tipped fingers

tightening round her bare ankle
        and the little vein mesh there
    the blood delta
        pale lavender.

*

When he has made his point
he collects and removes himself to the spare room
    as ordered
the soft-lit   oak-panelled
    low-ceilinged spare room.

Here he prepares himself.

He takes time
    shaking out creases
from his new white shirt with the jabot collar.

He sounds   with all he dares of his weight
    the nervous springs in the high bed.

He begins to imagine

    or will it be her room.

*

A knock
    the polite wood-knuckle sort.

Juliet.

Has she   what
        has she
changed her mind.

Is it now.

Then the door creaks and
        he sees not Juliet
Juliet's mother
    and the look of her makes his smile
            stiffen.

He thinks
                is she
    peering into his head.

    Is she   about to forbid.

But that would not explain why
        she is crying.

    It would not explain why
        she is wiping tears from both eyes
pinching her nose as if she might sneeze
    dimpling the eiderdown with her fingertips
            the silvery blue eiderdown
            stitched into lumpy waves
to occupy herself with the patterns she makes.

                    *

    A grown woman
            talking as she is crying.

Like suffocation.

                    But she does say clearly enough
                methodical for a moment at least
        his father has called on the telephone.

His father has called
                and his father.

        He interrupts.

With the inspiration of dread
                a mind-burst
        like a sapling
twigs   branches   quick green flickering
        instantly becoming a tree
                he tells her   he already knows
                    what she has to say.

And true
        there is nothing like surprise in his voice.

        Brain juddering.

                    Turbulence.

        But even that soon settles down
the air he breathes becoming perfectly smooth and
        steady again
                and him dry-eyed

at one remove from himself admittedly
        watching himself
as Juliet's mother tells him

          squinting at her watch
                    restraining the frilly white cuff of her blouse

his mother now
          just exactly now in fact
                    as they are speaking

his mother is in surgery because

          she is still not looking at him
                    she is still studying her watch

his mother is in surgery at St John's Hospital in
     Chelmsford
          where his father has already arrived.

Because of the accident   he tells her impatiently
          and wants to add
                    but does not add
               takes pity on her
                    as she backs away to the door
               both hands covering her mouth
adds to himself at least

          he has expected this all his life
feared would be better
     he has feared this all his life
and the only surprising thing
          but he cannot say this
     the only surprising thing is

          he wants to know more than anything
                    where Juliet is
the corridor   her room   waiting

not waiting any more
how could she be
waiting
or him
how could he wait for her
after this.

*

But they do go to the party.

It is explained
he cannot return home
there is no one

and his father
Juliet's mother says
his father thinks the party will stop him

what

worrying.

He doubts very much
worrying is the word
and that
is another thing he will not say.

Instead
he will do as his father wants.

He will   because of this
            seizing the new word   new to him
                        injury.

                        *

        He tries it again under his breath
                injury
when Juliet's mother ushers him
                injury
        and Juliet out of her car at the party
                then spins away
                        in a red-flare exhaust-ghost snow-flap

                relieved
                he understands

while he and Juliet
        not escaping the icy lunge
                of a magnolia hand by the front door
                        injury
so he is soaked along the left arm of his new white shirt
                    the shirt his father hates

while he and Juliet
                    duck into this stranger's house
        he thinks might not even exist
except as a stack of crammed and shining rooms
        bolted together with injury
                with bars of very loud music.

                        *

In the emptied-out dance room

empty apart from the Stonehenge sideboard
        which will never be the same again
                after that fag-end gouging a ruby furrow

in the space-trip spangling disco ball light

        in the profound heat
                    and rock-thrash

he must tell everyone
            he has this new distinction
        at the top of his lungs if necessary.

His mother is dying   probably
            even as he stands here.

        His mother is dying.

But the room   the entire house
        decides this is not important
                and the music drowns it.

The music   the dancing
        the talk of nothing
                    of everything but.

Juliet will not have it either.

        She is under orders
        and motherly a bit.

He must be cheerful
he must be occupied
he must be distracted.

So

here she is now   refilling his drink
here she is now   introducing him
here she is now mouthing his name
here she is now finding a side room
and settling herself   onto his knee
on both knees now   in his lap
with her   slippery weight and heat
moulding him through the dusk-red
satin trousers she has made herself

and

in the run-up to midnight
after someone has dimmed the lights

in the maze of a slow song

fatuous lyrics   he can hear that   fatuous
but who cares

laying her long bare arms on his shoulders
allowing him to breathe
the sleepy vanilla scent in the crease of her elbows
linking her fingers behind his neck
resting her forehead on his forehead
her black hair
her skin sealed to his skin

                as if her thoughts could fill him
                        as if she could flood him
with the perfect blank of her superior happiness.

                                *

It is embarrassing
                or something
when they slither into the deep cracked back seat
        of her mother's Rover
because at midnight sharp she has come to collect them.

He wishes the meat of his neck and shoulders
        were bruised by the weight of Juliet's arms.

He wishes his whole body had scorched
        when she nested on his knees
                in her sleek satin.

He wishes his mind had received her mind
        like a lake swallowing the stream that feeds it.

He wishes.

                And yet.

Although they are leaning together holding hands
        welded in the sublunary capsule of the car
he discovers after a mile or two
        Juliet is not noticeable to him.

        Not really.

Not compared to the silence
            hardening between the three of them
as witch trees weave their way home into a tunnel.

Not compared to the doubly darkened air
            sharpening polar blue dots
                        and pin-prick foxy eyes
in the fuel gauge and speedometer.

Not compared to Juliet's mother sparking a cigarette
            then milling open her window
                        the smoke tugged outside
                                    like a streak of chalk
while at the same time
            allowing shavings of the night flying past them

to curl in
            pure   sharp

despite the blurry cigarette whiff
            which he discovers
gives him a feeling of drowning
            of sinking below the frozen surface of the world
but also of rising
            of becoming a ghost himself

until   when he turns his head
            now ignoring Juliet entirely
he sees in the tunnel of the lane behind them
            in the tail lights
where gravel flares under the narrowing branches

a wreckage trail
                    made of his mother's possessions
          her riding jacket   her red collar
          her jodhpurs   her sheepskin slippers
          her Teasmade   her *Ring of Bright Water*
          her pair of pretend tortoiseshell hairbrushes
                          and mirror
          her stock   her gold pin with the fox mask
          her black velvet hard hat
her whole wardrobe of everything in fact
                    not much for a life
vanishing along with the moment he sees it
                    as the pasty clay hand stretches
from underground and grabs.

                              *

The Rover whooshes in
        between what must once have been gateposts
the gate itself long gone
            as Juliet's mother flicks her cigarette
out through the window crack
            and winds the handle backwards.

The cold stops at once.

The snow
            slows down.

The snowflakes in the headlights
        cleverly assemble
            into a swivelling cone
                centred exactly on him.

He deliberately resists
        their attempt at hypnosis.

He sees the cigarette bounce once on the gravel
    fizz
        and shrink to a glowering red eye
            that keeps watching.

*

When Juliet's mother has parked her car in the garage

when he has climbed out
    into the rank petrol stink
        the suicidal exhaust fumes

when he has negotiated
    the child's sleigh   spare tyre
        Flit spray   garden hose
festooning the walls

when they have slithered in from the snow blast
        to the shimmering kitchen

Juliet's mother reminds him he must be tired
    recommends Juliet to fetch him a glass of water
        and tramps upstairs
thinking she is doing him and Juliet a favour.

Her door eases shut at the far end
    of the long brown top-landing carpet with a sober
      click
        and he thinks no more about her.

He thinks almost nothing.

He has no room for anything.

He notices   instead.

He notices

    from the wicker dog basket
        creaks
as the dog   they have hardly been introduced
    a black Labrador
        sidles in from the hallway
      rotates once
and flops

    clock ticks
       from the moronic moon face
           beaming above the Aga

    house plant
        aspidistra is it   keep that
flying then
       stiff green flag shreds

    water
       the glass Juliet has brought him
misting on the kitchen table
    while he rubs the side of his thumb to and fro
       across the hysterical woodgrain
years of scrubbing have exposed as ridges

    Juliet
       leaning the small of her back against the sink
head down   face streaked by hair fallen forward again

shoes off
stretching her toes.

This silence   he thinks
                this silence
but he cannot complete the thought.

    A minute later
he drinks a mouthful of the water.

Another minute
    he says good night and retreats upstairs.

                        *

The moon peers at him
    over her neat cloud fold
and decides   it is time to change her orbit.

    She swings closer to the Earth.

    She whispers to him
in a white voice like ice fixing grass
    that now she has taken over the duties of the sun.

        That her bright light
                will shine by day
        as well as by night.

        And he accepts this.

He turns his face upwards
            and spreads his arms as wide as possible.

The moon in sympathy
          rests her entire weight
     on the shell of his chest.

He embraces her and
          she absorbs him.

                    He feels nothing at all.

                    *

Next morning the bus station is deserted.

     In the front seat of Juliet's mother's car he waits.

He asks himself
     what does the back of his head look like
          to Juliet behind him
     and has no idea.

               He waits.

     He breathes on the windscreen
               until gradually   patchily
          the mist tide retreats.

               He waits.

He thinks the concrete walls of the bus station sparkle
     or is that his imagination.

               He waits.

Certainly in his imagination
    he sees the Earth dangling
clear in the frost of its fatal winter
    in its epic and eternal lack of deliberate intent
    its brainless habit   not even habit
condition
    its condition of perpetual accident.

      He waits.

And when his bus eventually fusses into the station
    under the almost-too-low dry-blood-coloured steel
      girder
and other passengers materialise from the supermarket
  adjacent
    and from High Street patting snow off their over-
      coats
      he makes his goodbye.

      Not a kiss

    an embrace sort of for Juliet
      twisting over the seat dividing them

and for her mother a handshake
    which she rejects
briskly negotiating the steering wheel
    to smother then fling him away
      bundling his holdall after.

The car door behind him slams shut
    as the double door of the bus

      opens.

He steps towards it   the exact fare ready in his fist
        and the collar of his army greatcoat up round his
            ears
                tickling a bit.

    No need to show that.

Keep going
        OK.

            Pay
                OK.

                Turn OK
                    and wave.

                    *   *   *

In the car park of the White Hart
a neighbour   Mrs Hill   is waiting for him
    boxy in her boxy Land Rover.

He is thinking   if he is thinking
    the same as yesterday.

    Snow on the wind.

Glittering gravel glued together by frost.

The pub sign
    wincing in its frame.

Wham   wham   wham
    shuddering past on the A120.

Even the darker skewed tyre tracks
    carved by his mother's Hillman
        still present and correct.

At least Mrs Hill does not ask him
    how was the party.
                She avoids that pothole.

    Also   she has no idea about Juliet
and he will not say.

However   what can she tell him about his mother.

As Mrs Hill twists the ignition key
    hunches over the steering wheel
        and they kangaroo forward

she manages   mostly
        to keep control of the matter-of-fact voice
                she has evidently rehearsed all morning.

        His father has rung to tell her
        what the others had told him
        since he himself saw nothing.

        His mother's pony Serenade
        was jumping out of a copse.

        She pecked. His mother fell.

        She injured   she injured
        her head   and she lay
        unconscious.

                        An ambulance
        ferried her away to St John's.

        Today she is still unconscious
        after the operation last night.

        He will understand of course
        he cannot visit her   yet.

                        His father thinks
        that would not be a good idea.

He nods his own head   something is making him
                but he must
        why not visit her.

Mrs Hill delivers her answer
        as they curve down from the A120
                past the silage clamp
                        sulking under its black tarpaulin
                                weighed down with tractor tyres
        through the rip of the ford
beneath the chestnuts with snow congealed on their
    fingertips
                        and his mind jars open.

        Squat meringue ambulance
        flash light icy blue flash light
        mud concrete track his mother
        hard black velvet riding hat
        flung aside on a plough crest

        his mother high pillow bank
        yellow hair no hair shaved off
        succulent bruise red green-grey
        eyes shut eyes sunk eye sockets
        octopus oxygen mask clamping

        hiss hiss hiss hiss hiss hiss hisssss
        astronaut capsule open weightless
        bare surface dusty surface pebbly
        a planet no one has visited before.

                                *

His grandmother is rotating on the front step at home
        waiting to look after him.

To what.

His grandmother approaching eighty
  frail   deaf   incapable
   utterly perplexed.

  His mother is her daughter.

He reminds himself of this as Mrs Hill disappears
  elated he thinks like Juliet's mother
   she has done her bit
   and his grandmother offers her cheek
  a soft little rag of crumpled linen
   which irritates him
why   he does not want to think.

Except
  suddenly everything irritates him.

  Everything.

Pink hyacinths his mother propped upright
  with two grey knitting needles
   nevertheless swooning on the hall table.

TV advertising loudly in the sitting room
  to an audience of large empty chairs.

Swish of the dishwasher
  they never use that and anyway
   why at midday.

Most of all his grandmother's dog Janey
  hideous straw-stuffed overstuffed body
   hideous continual barking
  barking   barking   barking

and   come lunchtime
        when it is tethered by his grandmother
                to the leg of the dining-room table
        still barking   barking and lunging
dragging away the whole table and his plate with it
        as he aims his fork to stab
                cold ham and salad.

                          *

        He pounds upstairs to his bedroom
                and its gloom sanctuary
curtains permanently drawn even before today
                poster of Soft Machine
        glimmering as if it lived for ever
                        in the incense flicker of altar lights.

He has decided one thing.

        He has decided to anchor
                everything that remains
        in the continual stillness of remembering.

                Therefore
while his grandmother croons to herself in the spare room
                or Janey maybe
        he visits everywhere in the house
and examines objects in their places.

The ancient longways-splitting block of grimy soap
in the downstairs washroom used only by his father.

The picture in the hallway of a horse leaping over
a gate with the gate broken but the gate's shadow not.

The tile in the boot room representing the coat of arms
of the Bishop of Chelmsford for reasons he never
    fathomed.

The front door where at sunset with the temperature
    dropping
ice ticks faintly as it tightens on a puddle under the
    hawthorn.

The darkness   not an object
        it might as well be
the darkness back in his room again   the cube
    of safe air
        he thought it was safe
            the darkness now melting in silky strings
                    and droplets
        becoming atoms   prickling atoms
            buzzing and scooting
                colossal buffetings in nature
            but all mute all
                    mute
even the infinitely tall gas flame of his mother's scream
                    more silent
            than dust settling on moss.

                            *

Every evening now   seven or seven-thirty
        he loiters in his bedroom
and
        when his father's car leaps into the garage
                after his return from hospital
where he has stopped on the way from work

[40]

when the chrysanthemum glare of his headlights
        withers against the back wall

when his father's immaculate black London shoes
stamp across the tarmac to the front door
        at a military pace

he slinks down to the hallway.

He sees his father then
        head and shoulders wavering
through the two glass panels.

My father   he asks himself   my father
        have we met.

Dark grey London overcoat
                pale grey face
        hair white-grey at the temples
and head bowed under the dome of the outside light.

Merciless white light
        like the sun of a planet nowhere near to Earth.

His father pauses.

                        His father collects himself.

He pretends to wipe dirt off his shoes.

        Have we met.

Then he squares his shoulders and swoops indoors
        swinging his briefcase and

                    in a separate plastic bag
                                a dirty nightie
he extracts with a straight arm
            to whizz through to the laundry room
                                but not before
            its chalky talc smell
                            sweat smell
shit smell
            has scribbled its signature
                    the whole length of the hallway.

                                        *

            He is sent back to school.

He finds himself afloat
            in a new gravity
                        thinking about thinking
about living in sadness.

Everyone knows.

            Everyone
passes him around and between
            like a thousand-year-old
                        priceless manuscript.

And   despite them all
                despite himself
            he finds a new occupation.

He becomes Horatio in the spring play.

Not Hamlet.
Horatio.
Goodnight sweet prince.

His mother meanwhile
still floating herself
among the nebulae and gas clouds
of her vast unconsciousness
lands on the moon Pneumonia
where the inhabitants are lotus-eaters
where they dress in mist
where the delectable music
of waterfalls plays continuously
where she is welcomed with murmurs of affection
with kisses
where everyone who lives there
begs her to stay
and everyone looking on
from the far horizon of her hospital bedside
begs her to leave
himself included
when he is allowed to stand there
for the first time
which he understands
will probably be the last time

while his understudy takes over Horatio.

*

Nobody has told him
his mother has become epileptic.

But he sees for himself
when his mother has hauled herself back towards Earth
and his father allows him to visit
alone this time.

He tramps
an eternity of grey linoleum
with a high polish
hard-looking
but surprisingly cushiony underfoot
left   right   straight
left   right   straight
straight   straight   straight   straight
from the front door of St John's
to her ward in a Victorian block
squeezed between the incinerator and a laundry room
as a temporary solution to overcrowding
a hundred years ago.

He steels himself for a long look
at what he has so far only glimpsed
through a cordon of doctors and equipment.

For her shaved head with the stubble
no longer summery fair.

For the orange and red bruise on her temple
maturing to a dead colour
moleskin   trapped   dusty.

For the oxygen tank chipped silver
like treasure salvaged from a wreck.

For her face
     her chin-sag shark face
gaga   mouth hinged with saliva.

But when he arrives round the last corner
                    past the nurses' station
into the long ward
                    he sees none of this.

There is   his eyes panic
     there is her bed with her
          is this
with her curtain drawn

     with her floor-length pale blue cotton curtain
          twitching and bulging
and black wires   pulleys
     when he pokes his head through the slit

is this
          yes but pinned down   why
in a scrum
     why
          pinned down with four nurses
five
               and a doctor he must be
white coat
     biro scars above the breast pocket
          all of them trying
trying their utmost to
     weigh her down while her body refuses
               while her whole body leaps
like a trout dying in fresh air
               arching clear of the bed

slamming down
      devilish yellow bubbles now in her mouth
           lungfroth
feet dancing
      hands   smothering something
        or strangling

and
        the one in charge
      stethoscope round his neck
          red face
black-frame glasses knocked off his nose almost
      half twisting round without releasing his weight
not for a second
      staring him straight between the eyes
         bellowing

NOT NOW.

*

Grief
      too little a word
         no spring-lock inside it
primed
      to snap back to its opposite
   the second her eyes open   again.

   Sorrow   the same.

    Rage   the same.

Limbo then   limbo
    and better accept it.

[46]

Limbo.

    Better stretch out an idea
of life itself permanently stretched out
      touching its Michelangelo fingertips   just
against the outstretched fingers of death
    and vice versa.

                    *

In this way
    grief becomes
                the strange contentment
        of living in suffering
           without the possibility
of such unhappiness
        in whatever else
           remains of life.

Grief
      even providing a peculiar pleasure
              sometimes
   like the buzz a mind feels
when a tongue
        slides over a painful tooth.

Grief   whispering
         he will be content
    to live in a mirror-bright shining steel universe
      that can never be altered.

                    *

For three years the heat and dampness of her hand
        shit stink
              sweat stink
                  talcum sweetness
and equally that gargoyle stare
    or her eyelids
        tissue paper
    minuscule knotty purple veins
        fluttering   about to open
            never opening
only a fish dream
        rising to the surface
        to sip the light.

    For three years her beautiful thinness
        bloating into a big belly
    a flagon
pumped with drugs through a murky tube
    darting into the crook of her elbow
        also this other tube
            clear white
    into a hole in her throat
        through a metal ring
    that will not stop reminding him
of a washer on the pipe below the kitchen sink
    now they have taken her oxygen mask away.

For three years her palm skin and foot skin
    hardening into flawless alabaster

        the stifling hospital heat
sandpaper really

or the charcoal hands of the ward clock
          polishing her
whenever his back turns.

          And all the while nurses
     squeaking on their deep black rubber soles
          or nurses speaking very loudly
     checking her pulse
          honestly shouting
with never a reply
     never a word from her
not for his father   not for him
          gripping her hand
     absorbing the heat and dampness
                    which gave him life.

                    *

Then his mother opens her eyes.

     She looks
and the first thing she sees is somebody else's voice
     abandoned on the stony surface of the world
          she is now leaving.

     She picks it up
          and keeps on leaving.

She tries it out
     this battered trumpet
               these complex throat fingerings.

No.

      The voice is not hers.

      She does not recognise it.

      Nobody does
in this new world
          she means old
    where she is opening her rusty mouth.

      It is a husky monotone bass.

A throat wheeze.

      A cobwebbed twilit whisper.

But it will do.

It is good enough to blow strange sounds through.

     To ask   in so many words
        what happened
            what happened.
Can I come home now.

                *

He sits with her every day
    in the evenings his father.

It is their new order.

She speaks to him
          questions him rather
with googly eyes and between sleep-falls
     of disastrous depth and weight.

When he questions her
          her face mystifies.

She remembers light years away
          in miniature
     in a splintering dream tunnel
how he stretched towards her.

Or was that a moment ago
     and no one she knows.

One day he is an infant
     the next he becomes
          the same age as himself.

One day he seizes her attention
     the next his voice signal
          witters into infinite space.

He sits with her every day
     in the evenings his father.

                    *

A priest arrives
     someone his father knows
to conduct the service of the Laying on of Hands.

Behind the blue curtain drawn round his mother's bed
        with as much silence as possible
                in a ward at visiting time
                which is to say
with continual squawks   laughter   sobbing
        soft stream-murmurs of chat
chair scraping
        and thrashing in the curtains

                this priest steps forward.

He turns out to be an ordinary man in a suit
        and beneath the dog collar
                a black clerical shirt
        shiny with the impression
                of eternal washings and ironings
and a startling cream and yellow brocaded stole
        he whisks out of nowhere
then drapes around his neck.

He stoops
        and stares with his eyes shut.

He magics a prayer book
        and opens it with both hands
                cradling the floppy crocodile cover.

He murmurs
        as quickly as possible
                a silver stream tinkling over silver stones
embarrassed perhaps
        or is that devout.

And his mother

    he brings himself to look
just about
    at her blazing naked split-openness

        his mother lifts her face
    and her skin tightens
            her skin shines
    unearthly subcutaneous candle wax light
        as she devotes herself
            to the difficult work
    of concentrating extremely hard
on making her wish come true.

His father meanwhile
        at the foot of the bed
    clasping his hands together at waist height
and forgetting to hide
        as he usually does
    the forefinger he squashed
        in a deckchair as a child
his father bows his head
        to hide his wet eyes
and tears in the creases beneath his eyes
    and whatever he thinks.

For his own part
    he watches
            still.

He sees   at the appointed moment
    the priest lay aside his prayer book
rest his right hand

    no press   press his right hand
   no both hands   left piled on right
liver-spotted
   hard onto his mother's forehead
     which burns under the weight
        and ask God
  to enter her.

Lazarus he thinks
  in the second before
     this really is   more than ever
     intensely embarrassing
  in the second before
     this intense embarrassment
     might be an intervention
     as likely as anything
     to kick-start his mother's rigid body
     a body already dead
     before the mind has left it
     and the heart stops

in other words not.

          *

He wheels his mother's stretcher
  out from her ward to a corner of the hospital garden
summer grass yellowish between robust clover clumps
  and they sit quietly together
    as mother and son.

Their talk swerves   they like that
  their talk exists again now   and it swerves

but what holds him
        what he cannot avoid coming back to
is the hospital boiler in the shed opposite

    a shed with the wall facing them replaced
        by a single large sheet of glass
to expose the boiler inside.

A boiler   beautiful in its way
    painted valuable silver
            the deep-chested central drum
            dozens of tubes
            offshoots
            returns
            pipes
            drains
            eruptions
all of them shimmering
        the faces on dials
the luxurious flanks
                the dangling and twining arms

    all of them shining like the entrails of a body
housed and cherished outside that body
        and with no ceremony

as discreetly as possible in fact

        in a backwater garden
where no one in the course of a whole long afternoon
    comes to do so much
            as open a stopcock   or read a gauge
                or polish a drum

simply pursuing its business

hissing sometimes
emitting occasional clicks and whirrs
yawning extravagantly

pursuing its business while he and his mother
meander this way and that
this way and that in their talk together

until the light fades

and shadows crawl out of the black grass
to consume them

and dew falls

and he has no choice   except to wheel his mother back
and leave her at her place on the ward.

*

On Sunday mornings he and his father
collect his mother
in the Ford Transit christened Billy
ducking and rolling on the Chelmsford road.

It is hilarious
terrifying he should say.

No one outside the van could possibly know
how precarious she is   his mother
how brittle   how eminently
smashable

tethered by a flimsy seat belt
        a joke
    in the long shiny-floored metal back of the van
    where   if they braked suddenly

                she would rocket forward
        feet first
    through the shattering windscreen
her brokenness everywhere
                    breaking.

    The thought of it keeps them desperate
for the emptiness to stretch
            and last
                all the way home
                    with no interruption

            soft fawn club-headed grasses
                    curtseying at the curbside

            tyres burbling on sweetly

no interruptions
    except sunlight and tree shadow
            pouncing through the windows

and all the green traffic lights agreeing to let them pass

until they swing off the A120

            the White Hart
            in its childish hollow
            there to the right
            red tile roof

                    gravel car park
                    still exactly the same

and slow down through the village
        checking the church tower as per
                knapped flints flashing their glossy hearts
                    and bright chalk rims and seams

            the village shop Tea Rooms
                    the old Red Lion   now Rufus Leo a house
            always worth a smile

pass the tonsure of the new golf course

                    and so reach the turning circle
            the whispery tarmac outside the front door

            and stop

in the blunt shade of the empty extension
        built at great cost
                where the nurse never
                    where his mother never

and unload his mother onto the van's tail-lift
        squealing under her weight
                engine grudging
        but up to the job just

while a breeze across the ponies' field frisking
    the chestnut tree
                the tree with the downward-swooping branch
                    and patch of shiny bark
                where Serenade scratches her back

while a breeze
            flaps away the talcum smell
                        nearly

    and he and his father
            inch   squeeze
fiddle his mother's stretcher
    through the front door just
            very tight
                    breathe in
they say it every time
                    breathe in
    to the hallway and then with a lah-di-dah
make a laugh of it
                    four-point turn
            enter the sitting room

park her by the fireside
            busily shuffle up a side table
                    set her orange juice there
her pill-bottle battalion

        then   whoosh
            deflate on the sofa
and prepare to talk.

                        *

    He conducts an experiment.

Leaving at the end of visiting hour
    he hammers with his heels
            on the exploding-flower-head carpet tiles

of the corridor to the car park
and sees their blooms
shrivel a little
under the assault of his weight.

He makes as much racket as he decently can
clearing his throat
calling goodbye to the nurses
whistling a merry tune
so his mother will think him gone.

Then he tiptoes back
and peeps round the doorframe.

He sees
which he expects and dreads equally
her head sunk down
on her wafery breastbone.

He sees her eyes
not shut   her eyes blank
blind blue discs
like a statue staring.

He sees her
not herself.

Not present in herself.

He sees her willing herself
to drop through
the detestably tough skin of the world.

*

With no warning

after an arithmetic of years
    he has no reason to think
        are about to become the final amount

pneumonia visits his mother again.

    Pneumonia is a sly one he knows that.

        Pneumonia introduces itself
    as his mother's old friend.

It slips in at her mouth
    when none of the doctors are looking
and curls up inside her
    comfortable as a pussycat dozing.

Then it wakes up and he hears it.

    The growling catarrh.

But his mother.

When he looks into her eyes
    nothing looks back at him.

    She has already heard the delicious promises
        and fallen for them
           why not
        after a very long time.

She has already seen the radiant centre of the world
    where she is free to rise again
        exactly as needed.

As for him
      he thinks he understands completely.

He thinks for the time being
      there is nothing more he can say.

*   *   *

He remembers   at his mother's funeral

while he is watching his father at her graveside
   his father with smears of Essex clay
      yellowing the heels of his highly polished shoes

his mother telling him
   when his father was a child himself
daydreaming in his bedroom one white afternoon
   he hooked his feet underneath his metal bed rail
      rested his elbows on his knees
         cupped his chin in his hands
so that when his feet slipped and his hands shot upwards
      snapping his mouth shut
    he bit off the tip of his tongue.

What else could he do
      he remembers his mother continuing
   what else could he then do but spit it out
    and carry it carefully downstairs
  to his own mother in the kitchen
     and explain what had happened.

And what else could she do
   but drive to the doctor and ask him
     to sew it on again.

     To save the tongue and make it good as new.

PART TWO

Since they buried his mother
his father has moved   two hundred yards
        and gone to ground himself
in the humid labyrinth fox-earth of a farm cottage
            defended by beech hedge fortifications.

He has retired from human friendships
    and grown close
                to television.

He has poled himself with his ashplant
    thumb cocked in the polished cleft
        through every conceivable weather
most tellingly rain
        to the churchyard and bowed his head
with the same bafflement at her grave
            as the empty grass gap waiting beside it.

In this way thirty years have passed
    twenty-eight to be precise
            and now his patience has been rewarded.

His father has eaten his breakfast
    of one soft-boiled egg and white toast soldiers
        balanced a mug of tea into his study
and begun what he has to say.

*

In the bedroom of a house in north London
    he is dressing after a shower
        watching as it happens
           dreaming really
    how January daylight gaining strength
        seems to flex

    to roll in subtle almost-invisible waves
        between the lime tree branches
black lime tree branches spotted with white fungus
        latticing his window.

When the telephone rings
        the definite note in his father's voice
        takes him aback.

Bone cancer   his father announces
    shouting softly into the receiver
        poised a good three inches
           away from his mouth.

It is for him a confident start
    but leads nowhere.

A moment later his father has braked hard
    and peers
           teeteringly
    over the cliff edge of his own news.

In the pause
    in the ethereal
        crackling
           vertiginous
    air corridor that opens between them

he imagines his father
                    like a soldier on point
      whose duty is to reconnoitre
          hostile territory ahead.

He pictures him
      frowning over his desktop
            cleared for battle except
                  there is still the question
            of his violated pink blotter
                        with its cryptic mirror writing.

      Over the front lawn
            crew-cut to a bristling softness.

      Over the clenched metallic stubs of rose bushes
                  in two symmetrical beds.

      Over the beech hedge
            wintering as scraps
                  of mysteriously blank brown paper litter
                        skewered on twigs.

      Over the lane
            where car tyres have battered a loaf
                  of green horse dung into the gravel.

      Over the stubble field and ragtag crows
            picking through the remains
                  of a dead flint giant.

Until he arrives at good cover
      the horizon-wood
                  the Ashground

where he tries to avoid remembering
                    thousands of bluebell bulbs
hoarding their extravagant and ravishing colour tide
                    under a camouflage of wet leaves.

                              *

On the train
        immediately his father is allowed visitors
the caverns of Liverpool Street
                the brilliant moss ledges and lumps
        lighting the cindery brickwork
                might as well not exist.

Fenchurch and Stratford   Witham and Shenfield.

        Then the draggle and widening light
                above childhood flatlands
                    that still bewitch him
with their marvellous corals
                and Elvis-quiffed fish
            invisible to everyone except himself.

In the surprise of this haste
                he wonders under his breath
could it be ending now
        this eternal interval with his father
                this lifetime of silence.

Throttled
        that would be one word
                for both of them as bad as each other.

Choked   he admits
by their spitting resemblance
                        their
          actually rather relieving
                violent differences of opinion.

At the very idea
                a sensation like sea water
seeping through dry sand
                        consumes him.

He stares off
          through the quivering carriage window.

He dreams up
                a superbly powerful blade
          say the scimitar
                Boudicca forged onto her chariot wheel
hacking down perfectly easily
          without the least tremor of resistance
                        every Roman soldier track-side telegraph pole

          one-at-a-time
                one-at-a-time
                        one-at-a-time
                                one-at-a-time

  as his train sways woozily forward
          and by magic escapes
                the snake-mess of wires
  and failed conversations
                        seething in his wake.

                                *

His eagerness flabbergasts him
            considering he cannot decide yet
                exactly why it exists.

It even survives
            in fact it loves and guzzles
the sweaty air cocktail that envelops him
                the second he revolves
            into the spinning lobby of St John's.

St John's the same
            where they whisked her in
from the midwinter rush-hour hullabaloo
                and Christmas tinsel
            drooping in shop fronts

    then re-dressed her
in washed-out hospital greens
            acquainting themselves in the process
                with her blossoming wound
            her mouth
hanging not quite

                dead already.

                    *

He stops himself there   this time.

He concentrates instead on his father
        launching himself
                into the old corridor maze
                    cautiously for the first few steps
            then allowing a sudden and rapid sweep forward

this way
      this way   this way
that way
          this way

    afloat on the swirling blue linoleum
he half remembers

   taking in   sort of
hotspots where gull-nurses
         gaggle over a titbit

   four five six
        rigid sour yellow plastic doors

    blurred bed-row glimpses

   dozens at least dozens
       of visitors crouched over listening
   or offering

     a cubbyhole for Plant

a clichéd gurney
   rattling its white-as-a-sheet patient
     hell for leather
        and a doctor in hot pursuit

before idling into a backwater
     slowed
       like debris ushered aside from a flood rush
   to inspect
      whether he likes it or not

a long white art gallery wall
        Yorkshire terrier   cottage garden   tabby
            Ravello   onions   sunset

before
        finally
                delivering him.

                            *

Ah
        but he has caught his father at a bad moment.

His father   in a chair at his own bedside
        is decked in a stylish
                but sadly only knee-length
            dark-green paisley dressing gown
peculiarly like his own
                and bowed forward with his back turned
                        head to head with a doctor
                who has questions he must answer.

He tiptoes closer
        so far still invisible
                to his father at any rate.

The doctor   half his age
                            flustered
        flicks him a look
through heavy black-frame Eric Morecambe glasses

                realises
                        this must be a son

nods fractionally
                    and continues.

Your work   he asks his father.

    His father cannot remember.

Your middle name.

    His father cannot.

Your birthday.

    His father cannot.

Your regiment.

    His father cannot.

At which point
    he slinks forward
        until his father glimpses him
    in the fish-bowl curve of one lowered eye
turns full face
                    and smiles.

    His father knows one thing then.

And another
            it turns out.

Who is prime minister
    the doctor asks.

BLAIR

     his father spits it out
          as far as possible

BLAIR.

           *

When it is quiet again

     when they are settled
among the murmurings that pass for quiet
         in a twelve-bed ward at visiting time

he feels himself weightless and flying
     on the thermal of what he might call
         his own kindness.

But no.

     It is not kindness.

It cannot be kindness since
     it is not aware of itself.

     It simply exists.

He is a son and
     this is his father   and
         questions at least
    are finally possible between them.

To prove it he asks his father
          what
          has he
          really
          forgotten.

His father raises an eyebrow
     and steers his attention off
               through the wide end-window of the ward
          to contemplate a red brick water tower
that happens to glower over the hospital hinterland
     while scratching idly with his right hand
          black beetle therapy scabs on his left arm.

     See those pigeons.

                    He sees them
regular as a posting of sentries
     around the battlement of the water tower.

More than this
     his father will not say.

                    *

Next day
          which is the first day
of their new existence together
     he is still in the trance
          of this new gift he was born with.

     He exerts himself with no effort
     to engage his father's mind.

He drags forward the computer screen
        on its nifty retractable arm
                until it hovers close to his father's chest
    and explains the internet.

His father will not believe
    such a thing is humanly possible.

        You
        mean
        the
        whole
        world.

He shows photographs of his children
        and a vaporous paraffin flame
trims in his father's eyes
        then flops in a cross-breeze.

He dredges and displays
    scenes from his childhood mothering dream flow
but his father was seldom there
        and will not pretend to remember.

He pulls up a different screen
                a talk-screen
    of their rare and valuable excursion
their trip in June 2004
    through the lanes of Normandy
        where his father fought after D-Day.

    Here for a moment
they do sit down together
    with sun toasting their backs

among outrageously large and bright yellow buttercups
        in the very field where Colonel Gosling
                that would be Mike Gosling
                        i/c a half-track
came face to face with a Panzer
                and

        but his father forgets

                        he presses refresh

but his father

                        he presses refresh

but his father.

                                *

                Next day and the next
        when he turns the corner into his father's ward
                and his father now bed-bound
                        rolls his marble head
        to see who   to see what
                new interruption
                might be approaching
        and smiles a child's innocent and complete smile
                of recognition and relief
        he feels himself a son
                        as never before.

Airless hospital air
                composed of laborious efforts to breathe
        continues to bubble under his wings.

Next day and the next
        it raises him off the clinging ground
    the clay that detains him.

He skims
    the treacherous white water linoleum
            pathway approach.

He scans the ward
            like an angel scouting the empyrean
                and halts at a vantage point
where the complete panorama of the world is visible
            and discovers it consists of nothing
        except his father here and now.

He dream-steps and descends
            to his father's blue plastic bedside chair.

He leans close to his father
            like a man in a lighted room
                    pressing his face to a window
to make the outside darkness see-through
            in the hood of his own head shadow.

Despite the gigantic
        giddying well-shaft drop
            he sees himself clearly in the depths
craning up to the moon of his own face
            and his mother
    a smear of bridal white.

*

In the light of this
            the chair beside his father's bed
                  the snub blue plastic bucket chair
with eminently breakable hollow black metal legs
            has become his one
                  right place on Earth.

                  Besides which
his father has decided enough is enough
      and crept   rolled
                  crept   rolled
dragged himself by minute degrees
      and titanic effort
                  across the interminable surface of his ice sheet
to reach the furthest coast of his bed.

      He has turned his back.

            He has confined himself to the window eye
shining in the head of the ward.

When he studies it himself
      adrift
in the almost invisible light current
            he sees as his father sees
      pigeons now and again
                  slide off their water tower lookout post
                        keep a precise formation
over rows of glittering dolphins
                  ploughing the hospital car park
then by consent
            return as they were.

                              *

Everyone without saying a word agrees

and St John's finds him a bungalow hospice room
        closer to home
                with   as it happens
                    a flowering pink cherry
entirely filling the window frame.

And indeed
        the colour overwhelms them both

                        father
                and son

flooding them equally with its blood pulse
                heat illusion
canopy   and soak-through
        while the warm air they breathe together
 sways in a sea swell
                and the breeze tousles.

Not that his father has anything to say about it.

The task of breathing
            now requires his complete attention

                and to address it

he has squared his shoulders
            and drawn himself up to attention
under the large and loose Aertex squares
            of a blue ventilated baby blanket.

            This discipline by his father
this precision

mesmerises him.

There is nothing
    he wants to hear more
        than the silence of his father's tongue

           not to mention this other
                new and ancient language
    lip sounds
throat sounds
    lung sounds
             guts.

Whole hours pass
    while he is perfectly content
to trace the blurred body contours that begot him
        the shapely legs that were good for dancing
              the well-proportioned chest
          concealing the silent heart.

He admires the long arms and nervous hands
    the jumpy hands
        that gave his father's heart away
that shook   that trembled
    that felt and showed the threat
          of every action the world demanded
            down to and including
        deadheading the roses.

He examines
        the sound-asleep hollowing face
          dreaming on its pillow bank

    and discovers it more and more nearly
          resembles his own face.

        Until with no warning
no swallow   no cough
          no stir of a nervous hand

his father opens his blue eyes
                their colour astoundingly
                        faded to pale cement grey
fixes him and whispers

          never be blackmailed.

                        *

          His invincible father.

When he leaves
          he slips clean
                through the washstand mirror.

          His invincible father.

                        *

The flint village church
        where his father's coffin lies
                all service long
                        in a pool of warm gules
                cast by the April sun
        through the fair breast of a window saint
the church
        blackmails the congregation.

    [84]

The sexton's spade in the churchyard
        which has removed the surface grass
                in delicately snarling curls
and opened the Essex clay
                    to a depth of six feet
        exposing black root-wires scrabbling for a hold
the spade
        blackmails the earth.

The priest with his swirling language of dust
        who is the first to throw   timidly
                a clutch of earth onto the far-down coffin lid
        then beckons him forward to do the same
                    which he does but kneeling
                        to make the fall
                        and thud less dreadful
the priest
        blackmails the grave.

He backing away from the grave eyeing the sexton
                who himself eyes these proceedings
from the dark flame of an ancient yew tree
        and trampling   almost
                    on the grave of his mother
he
        blackmails himself.

His mother who has waited thirty years
        for her husband to climb into the bed beside her
        and whose name has faced into the rain so long
its letters are now slivers of grey moss
his mother
        blackmails everyone.

None of which
      he thinks
   as he stumps up the incline of the village street
towards the wake in the garden of his father's cottage
      makes the slightest sense
    and will never.

PART THREE

After forty years Juliet emails him.

       Can they meet.

    He reads her message again   and again
          counts.

    Forty years.

Since their first   last   date
      and lamplight
sweating on those oak panels in her spare bedroom
    magnolia leaves
        pat-patting a leaded window.

    Four zero.

Since her slithering black hair
         creamy swimmer's shoulders
            her big soft wide
words still fail him
        mouth.

                *

He delays answering

        a minute
   is hardly decent.

Very well another
            drumming his fingers
then   clickety-click at the gallop

and   send.

                    *

St Pancras station   the Booking Office Bar
            which is her idea.

He arrives early like a fool
      giddy a bit
            thanks to his head-back stare
                  at the barrel vault roof
and sunset's lilacs and charcoals
            staining the many-coloured glass.

      Or are they ghosts of the steam age?

At any rate
            he expects to kill time
      inspecting John Betjeman
            coming or going or both
                  in his flapping bronze mac
                        trainspotting the Eurostar
            flyblown chisel-face of the future.

                    *

            But Juliet is before him.

It must be   Juliet
        trailing in one hand her overnight wheelie bag
                the other
            clamped to a mobile and why not
        husband probably
            in Paris already or wherever.

And why not.

        Except his disappointment exists
                and is frankly
    scandalous even to him.

                            *

Juliet   he remembers now
                        she told him
        is wearing dark glasses.

            Very big   black-framed
                        curved
        very dark dark glasses
    masking her face
                as far as possible.

        That is all he has time for.

        Bye   she says.
                    That is her first word.

    To the phone naturally.

Bye.

As her wheels trundle to a halt.

As he imagines himself replying
            when in fact he is silent
                        and staring.

Not the white hand
            smuggling her mobile into the slit
                        of a navy overcoat pocket.

Not the beautiful black bob
            grey at the roots.

Not the mouth
                        thinned under its lipstick twirl
            think of the millions of breaths
                        the words
smoking over her lips
                        think of feet wearing down a threshold.

He is staring
            at scars on her face.

            Scars dicing into her lips
                        little hairline fractures
                                    glaze cracks
                        fissures and faults
not faults no
                        scars.

What happened.

            These are his first words
                        after forty years.

What happened.

*

     Juliet's hair shakes
blooms in a bridling pony-toss
        then soothes
            and fits neatly again.

Therefore
     he pretends he has seen nothing
        and with a bluff enthusiasm
            which for all she knows
     is now his natural everyday manner
        steers her into the bar of the Booking Office
and round to a
        bloody miracle
           empty corner table
without another word spoken.

*

In their background
     departure times and destinations
        trudge through watery echoes.

In their immediate vicinity
     high-gloss woodwork   new olde England
    horse-brasses
      and everyone taking a breather.

     He follows suit.

He orders house white
        and the waitress who understands
                speed is the essence
    rattles it down
        in a profoundly nervous silvery ice bucket.

                    *

Juliet meanwhile
        eases her dark glasses
    a fraction along her nose
        and rests them on a pale skin-ridge
the main scar there
    to hide it.

She has no time to waste
    and without the least flourish or sidestep
        delivers a boiled-down
           recitative
namely   her life since last they met
           and parted.

    Au pair   marriage
    two children   girls
    living in   freelance
    films   documentaries mostly.

                    *

He shuffles his glass on the tabletop
        creased apparently
      with ghostly cloth wipes

and cannot prevent himself
    still looking
        when he thinks she is not looking.

    At her hair sweetly hooked behind one ear.

At her jittery ear stud on its plump little flesh-cushion.

    At her white throat   very white throat
        swelling when she swallows
in the shadowy collar V
                of her expensive black silk shirt.

At her surprising   forgotten
        blunt-tipped   almost square-ended fingers
    nails unpainted   milky suns
        rising from the cuticle.

                        *

Then his turn   he thinks.

    But that is not what she came for.

    She stalls him.

        She slips off her dark glasses
                and shows him her white face
naked.

                        *

If she told him a wild cat
        launching out of a pine forest

if she told him a lightning strike

        a firework

an alleyway bottle-end lunge

    if she told him a particularly sharp idea
        an idea like a star birthing
            the most brilliant idea imaginable
had shattered out of her brain
                through her left cheek
        engulfed her left eye
and scorched her mouth

        he would believe her.

But   a company car
    the M40 late at night
                darkness   rain
            and roly-poly down the embankment
outside High Wycombe

                High
        Wycombe

    which Juliet offers
            without him asking
he cannot accept
        and must.

                *

No sooner
        the wet tarmac rubber smear
            the barrier can-opened
        the mud gouge   the grass rip
the steaming hush and blue dashboard glow

        than his mother of course.

    His mother in her own seamless flash footage
head shaved gingery bare
            tiger-slash operation scar
    eyes pulpy   bruise-mashed
        oxygen   tank   tube   mask
            oxygen itself
pressing a skeletal finger to pursed lips

            sssssssssshhhhhhhhh.

                    *

Juliet fills her glass   his glass
    but for him enough.

            Enough.

If he had come with a plan.

    If he had ever   and he had
                he sees that now
    in corn-yellow soft focus.

If he had ever imagined they might.

        Then   shame on him.

Shame on him and
            why not just creep away immediately
       with his tail and whatever else
          tucked between his legs.

*

Which Juliet has no time for.

    She is watching the clock.

           She is insisting her point is not
only the accident   her point
     is after the accident
          she lay unconscious three days.

*

Midwinter fields
          no footprint
     among flint bones
          and bristly Essex clay lumps
no shadow
       the seething snow surface
          opening
    and closing its lacy arms.

*

Unconscious Juliet continues
          then awake but not

awake-awake   not
         herself.

More like a radio dial twiddling
picking on day one
      a French signal
and her voice speaking only French
      on day two
          her voice in English
                 with a French accent
      on day three normal
her everyday voice
      beaming back to her
    from the spangling gas-warps
          of infinite deep brain space.

*

A waitress at the table adjacent
    clears cutlery like glittery fish in a handful.

He meanwhile
      sponges up what he hears.

      He wrings out Juliet's languages
         and squeezes them into his own language
   storing them
      along with the car wreck
   the rain the rain the rain   the headlights
      stubbed in embankment plough.

Although   as the debris
      the confetti windscreen glass
         the smashed boxer's face fender

the car radio
               churning its exciting trash regardless
                 and   in the midst of it all
Juliet's silence
    her scarred face   her unconsciousness

        as the combined weight of this
   groans
   creaks
   scrapes
   sinks
   settles
        and enters his consciousness

he reminds himself
    Juliet is not his punishment.

        Not if he chooses.

*

At which point
    she arrives at the point
        that brought her here in the first place.

She tells him   at last and suddenly
    she can remember nothing
        of her life before the accident.

She explains
        having forgotten everything herself
her sister remembered
        she knew him once.

She asks him
     what passed   please
          between them.

She is in his hands
          she says.

*

He straightens
          to meet Juliet's eye.

To enter her eye and drop
          through liquid green-flecked chestnut brown
     into the dead centre.

Which is prepared to believe him.

     Which is waste land.

          A cat look
     I know you   do I know you
          remind me.

*

He deliberates.

     He weighs her featherweight weight.

And he lets her go.

He lets her life go
        and Juliet in their time remaining
    bare faced   dressed in her wounds
        leans forward
      to catch what he has to say.